ELEMENTARY GRAMMAR WORKBOOK 3

MURIEL HIGGINS

Longman Group UK Limited
Longman House, Burnt Mill, Harlow,
Essex CM20 2JE, England
and Associated Companies throughout the world.

First published 1983
Ninth impression 1988

ISBN 0-582-55888-3

Illustrated by John Millington, Lynn Breeze
and Technical Art Services

Set in 10/12pt Linotron 202 Palatino

Produced by Longman Singapore Publishers Pte Ltd
Printed in Singapore

CONTENTS

REVIEW	4	WILL HAVE	35
BOTH/NEITHER	7	SHOULD HAVE	36
ALL/NONE	8	WOULD HAVE	37
COMPOUND FORMS: SOME/ANY/ETC	9	IF (Conditional 3)	38
		PASSIVE	40
MAY PERMISSION POSSIBILITY	12	DEFINING RELATIVE CLAUSES	44
PAST PROGRESSIVE	14	INDIRECT QUESTIONS	48
IF (Conditional 1)	16	INDIRECT COMMANDS AND REQUESTS	51
WOULD	18	PREPOSITIONS	53
IF (Conditional 2)	21	PHRASAL VERBS	54
EXCLAMATIONS	24	NON-DEFINING RELATIVE CLAUSES	55
SO/SUCH	25		
PAST PERFECT	27	QUESTION TAGS AND SHORT ANSWERS	57
MUST/CAN'T (LOGICAL)	29		
INDIRECT STATEMENTS	31	TOO/EITHER	58
USED TO	34	SO/NEITHER	59

REVIEW

1 Do you know these people? Have you met them before?

Kate   Tom   Rose and Nick   Angela   Per

What were they three years ago? Complete the sentences

1   _____Kate_____ _____was_____ a music teacher.

2   _____ and _____ art students.

3   _____ worked in a bank.

4   _____ _____ a schoolgirl.

5   _____ _____ an engineering student.

2 What did they want to be? Write sentences

bank manager	art teacher
engineer	architect
ballet dancer	concert pianist

1   Tom   _wanted to be a bank manager._ _____

2   Kate   _____

3   Angela _____

4   Nick   _____

5   Per   _____

6   Rose   _____

3 Ask and answer

1 Tom/bank manager? (Yes)   *Has Tom become a bank manager?*

   Yes, he has. He's a bank manager now.

2 Angela/ballet dancer? (No, drama student) _____

   _____

3 Kate/concert pianist? (No, music student) _____

   _____

4 Nick/architect? (Yes) _____

   _____

5 Rose/art teacher? (No, photographer) _____

   _____

6 Per/engineer? (Yes) _____

   _____

4 Write paragraphs

1 Nick/left college
   went to US
   /found a job/
   stayed there
   /lives in Arizona now
   When Nick left college, he went to the United States.

   He found a job, so he stayed there.

   He lives in Arizona now.

2 Per/went back to Norway/got a job in Oslo
   /didn't like it/left
   /works in Bergen now

   _____

   _____

   _____

   _____

   _____

3 Rose/left college/went to Italy to study
/decided to become a photographer/came home
and looked for a job
/works in Cambridge now

_____

_____

_____

_____

_____

4 Kate/25/decided to stop teaching
/wanted to study music/went to Germany
/lives in Hamburg now

_____

_____

_____

_____

_____

5 Complete the paragraphs about Angela and Tom

¹ *When* Angela ² _____ fifteen, ³ _____
grew very tall. She wanted ⁴ _____ become
⁵ _____ actress, ⁶ _____ she went to drama
school. She ⁷ _____ a student in London now.
When Tom ⁸ _____ twenty-six, his bank
sent ⁹ _____ to the north of England. He's
the manager of a bank ¹⁰ _____ a small
town called Crossley now.

6 What are they now? And where do they work or study?

1 Kate   *is a music student. She studies in Hamburg.* _____

2 Nick   _____

3 Angela _____

4 Rose   _____

5 Per   _____

6 Tom   _____

BOTH/NEITHER

1 Complete the sentences with *Both . . . and* or *Neither . . . nor*

	THREE YEARS AGO	NOW
Rose	student	photographer
Nick	student	architect
Angela	schoolgirl	student
Kate	music teacher	student

1 ___Both___ Angela ___and___ Kate are students now.

2 ___Neither___ Rose ___nor___ Nick had jobs three years ago.

3 _____ Nick _____ Rose have jobs now.

4 _____ Kate _____ Angela were students before.

5 _____ Rose _____ Nick were students then.

6 _____ Rose _____ Nick are students now.

7 _____ Angela _____ Kate are studying at the moment.

8 _____ Kate _____ Angela have jobs.

2 Write sentences about yourself and someone you know

Both (name) and I Neither (name) nor I	are have like can	. . .

_____

_____

_____

_____

_____

_____

_____

_____

_____

_____

ALL/NONE

1 Write sentences with *All* or *None*

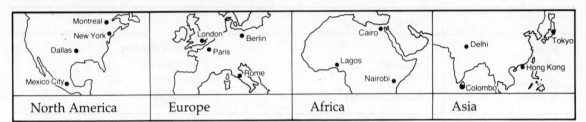

| North America | Europe | Africa | Asia |

1   Montreal, Dallas, Mexico City
_____ *All of these cities are in North America.*

2   Dallas, Nairobi, Tokyo
_____ *None of these cities are in Europe.*

3   Delhi, London, New York
_____

4   Nairobi, Cairo, Lagos
_____

5   Delhi, Tokyo, Hong Kong
_____

6   Paris, Berlin, Montreal, Cairo
_____

7   Berlin, London, Rome
_____

8   New York, Colombo, Lagos
_____

2 Find the right answer from the table

Both Neither All None	of them	are	near the sea. capital cities.

How are these
cities similar?

1   London and Paris? *Both of them are capital cities.*

2   Montreal, New York and Dallas? *None of them are capital cities.*

3   Dallas and Delhi? _____

4   Mexico City, Lagos and Tokyo? _____

5   New York and Rome? _____

6   Paris, Dallas, Cairo and Nairobi? _____

COMPOUND FORMS: SOME/ANY/ETC

1 Complete the conversation

IN AFFIRMATIVE STATEMENTS	someone somebody	something	somewhere
IN NEGATIVE STATEMENTS	anyone anybody	anything	anywhere

Rose lives in Cambridge now. She shares a flat with a girl called Jan. It's 6.30, and Rose has just come home from work.

ROSE   Hello, Jan. Were there any letters for me today?

JAN   Hi. Yes, there was [1]___*something.*___. I didn't get [2]___*anything,*___, but there was certainly [3]_____ for you.

ROSE   A bill, I expect.

JAN   No, it was a letter. Now where did I put it? [4]_____ in the kitchen, I think. But I can't see it [5]_____. Ah – there it is, on top of the fridge. I knew I put it [6]_____ in here.

ROSE   Thanks. Oh, it's from America. Dallas, Texas! But I don't know [7]_____ in Texas.

JAN   Well, [8]_____ must know *you*. A Texan millionaire, maybe.

ROSE   No, unfortunately I don't know [9]_____ who's a millionaire. (opens the letter) Oh, it's from Nick. Of course, he's in Texas on holiday.

JAN   There! You know [10]_____ in Texas after all!

ROSE   . Well, I don't know [11]_____ who actually lives there.

2 Do YOU know anyone who . . . ?

> Yes, I know someone who . . .
> No, I don't know anyone who . . .

. . . lives in Texas?   _____

. . . has visited Texas?   _____

. . . is a millionaire?   _____

. . . often visits America?   _____

. . . speaks American English?   _____

. . . speaks several languages?   _____

3 Find the right ending

	someone who something that	gives heat and cooks food. helps to put fires out. uses a typewriter. prepares meals. prints letters and figures. contains chemicals to put fires out.
. . .		

1 A fireman ___*is someone who helps to put fires out.*___

2 A typewriter _____

3 A cook _____

4 A typist _____

4 A fire-extinguisher _____

6 A cooker _____

4 Complete the sentences with *some/any . . . else*

someone/body anyone/body	else	=	some/any other person
some/anything else		=	some/any other thing
some/anywhere else		=	some/any other place

1 Nick is the only person Rose knows in Texas. She doesn't know ___*anyone else.*___ .

2 For his next holiday, Nick isn't going to go back to Texas. He wants to go_____.

3 He'd like to visit Mexico, because he likes Mexican food very much. In fact, he never eats

_____!

4 It wasn't Rose who wanted Nick to go to America. It was _____.

5 Nick likes living in America. He doesn't want to work _____.

6 He sent Rose a letter, and _____, too: a photograph of himself in Dallas.

5 Answer *Yes*

everyone everybody	everything everywhere

1 Who have you asked to the party? All your friends? All the people you know?
Yes, I've asked everyone.

2 You can't find your favourite tape? Have you looked in your bedroom? In the living room?
_____

3 Have you bought all the food and all the drinks?
_____

4 Have you told all your friends your new address?
_____

5 Have you remembered all the things you wanted to do?
_____

6 You still can't find that tape? Well, have you looked under the table in the living room, and in the desk? _____

You haven't! Look, here it is in your cassette recorder!

6 Finish these sentences about yourself and people you know
(Remember to use the correct form of the verbs)

fly an aeroplane ride a bicycle visit (Australia)	drive a car ride an elephant . . .

No one in my family can _____

Everyone I know can _____

Everyone in my class wants to _____

Nobody in my class has ever _____

I don't know anyone who has ever _____

But I know someone who has _____

No one in our family likes _____

But everyone likes _____

MAY

PERMISSION

1 Find the right question

> Use *May I* to ask for permission to do something

	borrow wash close leave use ask	a question, the window, at 11.30, your dictionary, your hands, your telephone,	please?
May I			

1 You're in your English class, and you've found a word you don't understand. You want to look it up in a dictionary. *May I borrow your dictionary please?*

2 You're at a friend's house, and you want to phone your parents to tell them where you are.

_____

3 Someone is explaining something to you, but you don't understand very well, and you want to ask something. _____

4 You're in your classroom, and you're rather cold.

_____

5 You have to go to the hospital at twelve o'clock, so you want to ask for permission to leave early. _____

6 You've just arrived at a friend's house. You had to change a tyre on your car, and your hands are very dirty. _____

2 What do your parents say?

> Yes, of course you may.
> Well, perhaps you may.
> No, you certainly may not.

You ask:

May I buy a new pair of jeans?

May I go to England next year?

May I learn to drive soon?

May I invite six friends to stay?

May I cook a meal tomorrow?

May I watch TV till midnight?

They answer:

_____

_____

_____

_____

_____

_____

POSSIBILITY

3 Read the conversation, then write sentences.

> Perhaps I'll go = I may go.
> Perhaps I won't go. = I may not go.

ROSE   Nick wants me to visit him in Arizona!

JAN   Will you go, do you think?

ROSE   I don't know. Perhaps I'll go next year. (1)
I'll ask for a month's holiday, perhaps. (2)

JAN   But perhaps your boss won't let you go. (3)

ROSE   Maybe I'll leave my job, then. (4)

JAN   Don't do that! It'll be difficult to find another, perhaps. (5)

ROSE   Well, perhaps I won't want another job in England. (6)
Perhaps I'll stay in Arizona. (7)
Perhaps Nick and I will get married there. (8)

JAN   But then perhaps I'll never see you again, Rose! (9)

ROSE   Don't worry, Jan. I'm only talking about what *may* happen. It's not definitely going to happen, you know.

1   *Rose may go to Arizona next year.* _____

2   _____

3   _____

4   _____

5   _____

6   _____

7   _____

8   _____

9   _____

4 What about you?

What may happen? Remember, you're writing about things that are possible, not about things that are definite or certain.

Before I go to bed tonight, I may _____

Tomorrow _____

Next month _____

Next year _____

In 1999 _____

PAST PROGRESSIVE

1 What were they doing three years ago?

Kate		teaching music.
Tom	was	working in a bank.
Per		studying engineering.
Nick and Rose		studying art.
Rose and Kate	were	sharing a flat.

1 Nick was a student.   *He was studying art.*

2 Kate was a teacher.   _____

3 Rose and Kate were friends.   _____

4 Per was a student.   _____

5 Tom had a job.   _____

6 Nick and Rose were students.   _____

2 Ask and answer

1 Kate/teach/music or art

  Was Kate teaching music or art?

  She was teaching music. She wasn't teaching art.

2 Nick and Rose/study/art or music

  _____

  _____

3 Tom/work/bank or shop

  _____

  _____

4 Kate and Rose/share/flat or house

  _____

  _____

5 Rose/study or teach

  _____

  _____

3 What happened to Rose?

Poor Rose! She had a bad day yesterday. These things happened:

She took some photographs.	She met a friend.
She lost her keys.	She dropped her camera.
A bee stung her.	She hurried home.
They talked.	She got into the river.
She tried to find her camera.	She fell.

A Which actions lasted several minutes?

She took some photographs.

_____

_____

_____

_____

B Which actions happened quickly or suddenly?

She dropped her camera.

_____

_____

_____

_____

Write one sentence for each picture

1 While ___*she was taking some photographs, she dropped her camera.*_____

2 As _____

3 When _____

4 As _____

5 While _____

4 What about you?

What were you doing at this time yesterday?

_____

Where were you living a few years ago – in a house or a flat or somewhere else?

_____

Were you learning English then?

_____

Which school were you going to?/Where were you working?

_____

IF (CONDITIONAL 1)

1 Look and answer

What will you see . . .

1 . . . in front of you if you turn right? _The river._

2 . . . on your left if you go straight ahead? _____

3 . . . on your right if you turn left? _____

4 . . . on your left if you cross the bridge? _____

5 . . . in front of you if you turn left? _____

6 . . . on your right if you go straight ahead? _____

7 . . . on your left if you turn left? _____

2 Tell me how to get there

	_If_ + PRESENT TENSE		FUTURE
If you	turn right, turn left, go straight ahead,	you'll see it	on your right. on your left. in front of you.

I'm in River Street, and I want you to help me.

1 I want to go to the river.
   If you turn right, you'll see it in front of you.

2 Where's the railway station?

   _____

3 Can you tell me how to get to the Star Hotel, please?

   _____

4 Do you know where the market is?

   _____

5 I want to go to the Sports Centre.

   _____

3 These things will probably happen if . . .

1 You'll probably be safe
if you stay in your car.

2 You'll probably get an electric shock

_____

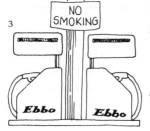

3 You'll probably cause a fire

_____

4 The dog will probably bite you

_____

5 You'll probably get into difficulties

_____

6 You'll probably get into trouble

_____

4 Complete the sentences with the verbs in brackets

1 I _____'ll give_____ you a present   (give)
if you ___pass___ your exams.   (pass)

2 If you _____ your exams,   (not pass)
you _____ repeat the course.   (have to)

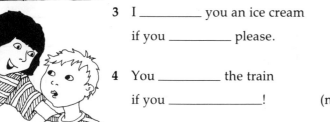

3 I _____ you an ice cream   (buy)
if you _____ please.   (say)

4 You _____ the train   (miss)
if you _____!   (not hurry)

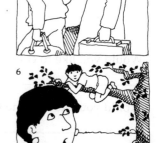

5 If you _____ well,   (not be)
you _____ to go to work
tomorrow.   (not be able)

6 You _____   (fall)
if you _____ careful.   (not be)

17

WOULD

1 Invite your friend

> Use *Would you like to . . .?* for invitations

GAMES	ACTIVITIES	PLACES TO EAT	GOING OUT
football tennis . . .	go shopping go swimming go fishing . . .	Chinese restaurant Indian restaurant . . .	go to the cinema go to the theatre go to a concert . . .

1 This afternoon you want to play a game.

Would you like to play _____ *this afternoon?*

2 You want to eat in a restaurant this evening.

_____

3 You want to arrange an activity tomorrow.

_____

4 You want to go out somewhere on Sunday.

_____

Now think of four more invitations

(tonight) _____

(tomorrow morning) _____

(next Friday) _____

(next weekend) _____

2 Accept or refuse these invitations

> Yes, thanks. I'd love to.
> No, I'm sorry. I'd like to, but I can't.

Would you like to come and have a meal at my house on Tuesday?

_____

Would you like to come to the theatre with us next Saturday?

_____

Would you like to go shopping with me tomorrow?

_____

3 Ask someone to do something

> Use *Would you . . . ., please?* for polite orders/requests

1 It's rather hot, and the window is closed.
   Would you open the window, please?

2 You want to borrow some money. (Careful! Who borrows? Who lends?)

3 You forgot to post your letters, and your friend is going to the Post Office.

4 You forgot to buy stamps, too. You want four stamps.

5 Your friend has just finished reading the newspaper, and you want to read it now.

6 Someone wants to speak to you on the telephone, but you're going out. You ask him to phone again later.

4 Choose something else

> Use *I'd prefer/I'd rather have* for preferences

You're in a restaurant with Pat. You're looking at the menu.

PAT   Now, what would you like? Chicken?
YOU   _No, I'd rather have _____ , please._

PAT   That's a good idea. Which vegetables shall we order? Peas?
YOU   _____

PAT   Right. Now, drinks. What would you like? Coke?
YOU   _____

PAT   Fine. I'll order that for you. And for dessert, what would you like? Ice cream?
YOU   _____

PAT   And I'd like that too. Now we can order. Waiter!

5 Can you answer these silly questions?

> JENNY I'd rather have measles than mumps
> PENNY I'd rather have mumps than measles.

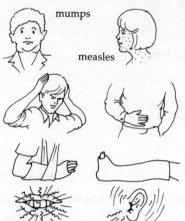

mumps

measles

Would *you* rather have mumps or measles?

_____

Would you rather have a headache or a stomachache?

_____

Would you rather have a broken arm or a broken leg?

_____

Would you rather have a sore tooth or a sore ear?

_____

(Of course, everyone would rather not have *any* of these!)

6 Now answer these more sensible questions with *I'd rather*

Would you rather . . .

. . . buy cheap food from a shop far away from your home,

or expensive food from a shop near your home?

_____

. . . work indoors or outdoors?

_____

. . . earn a lot of money in a boring job, or very little money in an interesting job?

_____

. . . work in your own country or in another country?

_____

. . . buy cheap clothes every six months, or expensive clothes every six years?

_____

. . . be a film star or a pilot?

_____

. . . spend all your money or put it in the bank?

_____

. . . visit England or the United States?

_____

IF (CONDITIONAL 2)

If + PAST TENSE		*would/could/might*
If	I had a lot of money, I was very rich, I became a millionaire,	I'd build a big house. I could buy an oil well. I might go round the world.

1 What would you do? What might you do?

If you had a lot of money, what would you do with it? What might you do? And what would you probably *not* do? Do you want some ideas?

build a big house buy an oil well buy expensive clothes buy gold and diamonds give it away	go on a long holiday travel round the world spend it all . . . . . .

Write sentences

Things I would do ___*I would*_____

_____

Things I might do ___*I might*_____

_____

Things I probably wouldn't do ___*I probably wouldn't*_____

_____

2 Answer the questions

If you built a house, where would you build it?
*If I built a house, I'd build it in*_____

If you gave the money away, who would you give it to?

_____

If you took a long holiday, where would you go?

_____

If you wanted expensive clothes, where would you buy them?

_____

If you wanted a car, what kind would you buy?

_____

3 Read this and then finish the sentences

Ken sees a burglar. He's going to phone the police.

The burglar has a gun. They're giving him everything.

The burglar's pointing his gun at them. They're frightened.

The burglar has left. They're happy.

The police are too late, and the man's very angry.

1 I'd phone the police, too, if _I saw a burglar._

2 I'd give the burglar everything, too, if _____

3 I'd be frightened, too, if _____

4 I'd be happy, too, if _____

5 I'd be very angry, too, if _____

4 What would you say?

Congratulations!	How do you do?	Excuse me, please.
Thank you very much.	Oh, I'm very sorry.	Don't worry about it.

1 What would you say if your cousin had a baby?

If my cousin had a baby, I'd say 'Congratulations!' _____

2 . . . if you stood on someone's foot by mistake? _____

_____

3 . . . if someone gave you a present? _____

_____

4 . . . if you wanted to go past someone in the next seat at the cinema? _____

_____

5 . . . if you met someone for the first time? _____

_____

6 . . . if your friend was very unhappy about an exam? _____

_____

5

What is your advice? What do you suggest?

> I'd . . . .* if I were you.

1 JAN I'm going to buy a new car.
(suggest a make or model of car: Ford, Metro . . .)

I'd buy a _____ if I were you. _____

2 ROSE I want to paint the living room. But what colour?
(suggest a colour)

_____

3 TOM I'm going on holiday. Where shall I go?
(suggest a country)

_____

4 KATE I have a headache. What shall I do?
(suggest something to help)

_____

5 PAT I want to see a good film.
(suggest a film title)

_____

6 ANGELA I'm hungry. What can I have?
(suggest something she can have)

_____

6

Complete the sentences with the verbs in brackets

Maria is a girl from your country. She's studying English and she'd like to visit an English-speaking country.

1 If Maria ____*went*____ abroad, she *'d go*_____ to England or America.   (go, go)

2 She _____ London if she _____ to England.   (visit, go)

3 If she _____ in London, she _____ a lot of money.   (stay, spend)

4 She _____ to stay for long if she _____   (not be able,

all her money!   spend)

5 If her holiday _____ very short, she _____ much English.   (be, not speak)

6 It _____ a pity if she _____   (be, not try)

to speak English.

---

* *if I were you* is a fixed idiomatic phrase used when giving advice.

EXCLAMATIONS

1 Find the right thing to say

What an idea!
What a coincidence!
What a lie!
What fun!
What a disappointment!
What luck!

Why aren't you going?
He probably spent it.
We can swim every day.
That's *my* birthday, too.
You always win prizes.
It's in the middle of a desert.

1 Let's go and live in Timbuktu.
What an idea! It's in the middle of a desert.

2 We're building a swimming pool.

3 I've won a prize in the competition.

4 Harry says he lost the money.

5 I'm not going to America after all.

6 My birthday's the ninth of September.

2 What do you think about these things?

How...!	I'd like I wouldn't like	to have a ... like that!

splendid pretty	ugly beautiful	interesting uncomfortable	lovely awful	nice . . .	terrible . . .

1 *How* _____ !
  I _____ *to have a hat like that!*

3 _____

2 _____

4 _____

SO/SUCH

1 Finish the sentences

> so + (adjective) that + (clause)

expensive cold fierce old heavy easy	we can't lift it. I'm going to throw it away. I'm not going to buy it. everyone is afraid of it. you need a scarf. everyone knows the answer.

1 The teacher's question is __so easy__
   that everyone knows the answer.

2 This dog is _____

_____

3 This chair is _____

_____

4 The TV set is _____

_____

5 That watch _____

_____

6 Today it's _____

_____

2 Complete the sentences

> so much + uncountable noun
so many + plural noun

1 Peter has ___so many books___ that he needs a new bookcase.

2 Mr Million has _____ that he can't spend it.

3 There are _____ in this family that
   they need a new house!

4 There was _____ yesterday that the road is flooded.

5 There are _____ in this room that it
   smells like a flower shop.

3 Finish the sentences with *such a* or *such*...

> such a + adjective + singular noun
> such + adjective + plural/uncountable noun

Freda is talking about her holiday

1 The water was warm. I've never swum in _such warm water._

2 The village was pretty. I've never seen _____

3 The people were friendly. I've never met _____

4 The restaurants were cheap. I've never seen _____

5 The food was delicious. I've never eaten _____

6 The hotel was comfortable. I've never stayed in _____

Only two things were wrong:

7 The beaches were busy. I've never seen _____

8 And the sand was very hot. I've never walked on _____

4 Complete the conversation with *so* or *such*

JAN   Tell us more about your holiday, Freda.

FREDA   We enjoyed ourselves [1]_so_ much that we didn't want to leave. Everyone was
         [2]_____ friendly, and they're [3]_____ helpful people too. We've never made
         [4]_____ many friends before.

JAN   And the weather was good, wasn't it?

FREDA   It was splendid. It was [5]_____ warm and sunny that we swam every day.

JAN   Was the water clean?

FREDA   Yes, and it was [6]_____ clear that you could see right down to the bottom. I've
         never swum in [7]_____ warm water, either. It was [8]_____ warm that we swam
         for hours.

JAN   What about the food?

FREDA   Well, there were [9]_____ many restaurants that we ate in a different one every
         evening. I've never had [10]_____ good fish. We ate [11]_____ much that we put
         on a lot of weight. Really, it was [12]_____ delicious that we never stopped eating!

JAN   I'm glad to hear you had [13]_____ a good holiday and enjoyed everything
         [14]_____ much. Maybe I'll go there next year.

PAST PERFECT

1 Which happened first

Read each sentence and decide which happened first. Then write A or B

	A	B	
1	I had reached home	when the rain started.	A
2	The rain had already started	when I reached home.	
3	The rain didn't start	until I'd reached home.	
4	When the phone rang,	I had just opened the door.	
5	The phone had already started to ring	when I opened the door.	
6	The phone didn't ring	until I'd opened the door.	
7	It had stopped ringing	when I reached it.	
8	I didn't reach it	until it had stopped ringing.	
9	I reached it	before it had stopped ringing.	

2 Find the right sentences

1 *The rain had already started when I reached home.*

2 _____

_____

3 _____

_____

3 Choose the right sentence from the box

1   Peter found a job before
    his father died.

When his father died, Peter found a job.
When his father died, Peter had already found a job.

When his father died, Peter had already found a job.

2   We bought the new house
    and then sold the old one.

When we bought our new house, we sold the old one.
When we bought our new house, we had sold the old one.

3   Mary started French
    and then went to Paris.

When Mary went to Paris, she had started French.
When Mary went to Paris, she started French.

4   The police arrived and
    then the burglar escaped.

When the police arrived, the burglar had escaped.
When the police arrived, the burglar escaped.

4 If only...

Use *If only* + past perfect about things that didn't happen

1   The police didn't come soon enough.   *If only they had come sooner.*

2   You missed the train because you didn't leave home early enough.

_____

3   You didn't walk very quickly.   _____

4   You didn't get up early enough.   _____

5   You didn't plan things very well, did you?   _____

(If you'd planned things better, you wouldn't have missed the train!)

5 What about you?

Have you ever wished that things had been
different? Perhaps you made a mistake or
forgot something. Write sentences.

If only I I wish I	had hadn't	...

_____

_____

_____

MUST/CAN'T (LOGICAL)

1 Complete the conversation with *must* or *can't*

Jan has asked some of her friends to dinner, and she's busy in the kitchen. Rose is looking out of the window. She doesn't know Jan's friends. Most of them are coming by car:

> Angela has a small green car.
> Brenda has a large red car.
> Chris doesn't have a car.
> Don has a small white sports car.
> Ed has a large green car.

ROSE   I can see a small car coming.

JAN   Then it ¹_____*must*_____ be either Angela or Don. It ² _____ be either Brenda or Ed. What colour is it?

ROSE   White. And it's a sports car.

JAN   It ³_____ be Don, then. Angela's car is green, so it ⁴_____ be her.

ROSE   Now there's a red car at the corner.

JAN   Red? Oh, that ⁵_____ be Brenda.

ROSE   Here's a green car now.

JAN   Good. It ⁶_____ be either Ed or Angela.

ROSE   What about Chris?

JAN   It ⁷_____ be Chris. He hasn't got a car. Is it a big car?

ROSE   Yes, quite big.

JAN   Then it ⁸_____ be Ed. Any more cars coming?

ROSE   Another green one, a small one.

JAN   Well, that ⁹_____ be Angela. She's got a Metro.

ROSE   Perhaps this is Chris now – a taxi's just arrived. Oh, a woman and a child are getting out. It ¹⁰_____ be Chris.

2 What do you think they must mean?

1   It says in this newspaper that London has a population of seventy million!

They can't mean _____ seventy million.

They must mean _____ seven million.

2   And it says the Alps are between France and Spain!

_____ the Alps.

_____ the Pyrenees.

3 It says Naples is in Sicily!

_____ Italy.

_____ Sicily.

4 And they talk about a film star called John Wine.

_____ John Wayne.

_____ John Wine.

5 And it says _Hamlet_ was written by Shookspur!

_____ Shookspur.

_____ Shakespeare.

Oh, I see! Now I understand. It's a competition. It says 'Can you find five mistakes on this page?'

3 What am I thinking of?

CANADA	AMERICAN	LONDON
PARIS	ATHENS	MADRID
OXFORD	CHINESE	GREECE
	ROME	

1 I'm thinking of a place.

It ___can't___ be ___Chinese___ or ___American___, because they ___aren't___ places.

2 It's a city.

It _____ be _____ or _____, because they _____ cities.

3 It has six letters.

It _____ be _____ or _____, because _____ six letters.

4 It's in England.

It _____ be _____ or _____, because _____.

5 The first letter is the same as the fourth letter.

It _____ be _____, so it _____!

ANSWERS

REVIEW

Ex 1 1 Kate was   2 Rose and Nick were   3 Tom
4 Angela was   5 Per was

Ex 2 1 Tom wanted to be a bank manager.   2 Kate
wanted to be a concert pianist.   3 Angela wanted to be
a ballet dancer.   4 Nick wanted to be an architect.   5
Per wanted to be an engineer.   6 Rose wanted to be an
art teacher.

Ex 3 1 Has Tom become a bank manager? Yes, he has.
He's a bank manager how.   2 Has Angela become a
ballet dancer? No, she hasn't. She's a drama student
now.   3 Has Kate become a concert pianist? No, she
hasn't. She's a music student now.   4 Has Nick become
an architect? Yes, he has. He's an architect now.   5 Has
Rose become an art teacher? No, she hasn't. She's a
photographer now.   6 Has Per become an engineer?
Yes, he has. He's an engineer now.

Ex 4 1 When Nick left college, he went to the United
States. He found a job, so he stayed there. He lives in
Arizona now.   2 When Per went back to Norway, he
found a job in Oslo. He didn't like it, so he left. He works
in Bergen now.   3 When Rose left college, she went to
Italy to study. She decided to become a photographer, so
she came home and looked for a job. She works in
Cambridge now.   4 When Kate was twenty-five, she
decided to stop teaching. She wanted to study music, so
she went to Germany. She lives in Hamburg now.

Ex 5 1 When   2 was   3 she   4 to   5 an   6 so
7 's/is   8 was   9 him   10 in

Ex 6 1 Kate is a music student. She studies in
Hamburg.   2 Nick is an architect. He works in Arizona.
3 Angela is a drama student. She studies in London.
4 Rose is a photographer. She works in Cambridge.
5 Per is an engineer. He works in Bergen.   6 Tom is a
bank manager. He works in Crossley.

BOTH/NEITHER

Ex 1 1 Both Angela and Kate   2 Neither Rose nor
Nick   3 Both Nick and Rose   4 Neither Kate nor
Angela   5 Both Rose and Nick   6 Neither Rose nor
Nick   7 Both Angela and Kate   8 Neither Kate nor
Angela   **Ex 2** (student's own answers)

ALL/NONE

Ex 1 1 All . . . North America.   2 None . . . Europe.
3 None . . . Africa.   4 All . . . Africa.   5 All . . . Asia.
6 None . . . Asia.   7 All . . . Europe.
8 None . . . Europe (NOTE After none — and neither in
Ex 2 below — is and are are both acceptable.)

Ex 2 1 Both of them are capital cities.   2 Neither of them
are capital cities.   3 Neither of them are near the sea.
4 All of them are capital cities.   5 Both of them are
near the sea.   6 None of them are near the sea.

COMPOUND FORMS: SOME/ANY/ETC

Ex 1 1 something   2 anything   3 something
4 Somewhere   5 anywhere   6 somewhere
7 anyone/body   8 someone/body   9 anyone/body
10 someone/body   11 anyone/body

Ex 2 (student's own answers)

Ex 3 1 A fireman is someone who helps to put fires
out.   2 A typewriter is something that prints letters and
figures.   3 A cook is someone who prepares meals.
4 A typist is someone who uses a typewriter.   5 A
fire-extinguisher is something that contains chemicals to
put fires out.   6 A cooker is something that gives heat
and cooks food.

Ex 4 1 anyone else.   2 somewhere else.   3 anything
else!   4 someone else.   5 anywhere else.
6 something else

Ex 5 1 Yes, I've asked everyone.   2 Yes, I've looked
everywhere.   3 Yes, I've bought everything.   4 Yes,
I've told everyone.   5 Yes, I've remembered everything.
6 Yes, I've looked everywhere.   **Ex 6** (student's own
answers)

MAY

Ex 1 1 May I borrow your dictionary, please?   2 May I
use your telephone, please?   3 May I ask a question,
please?   4 May I close the window, please?   5 May I
leave at 11.30, please?   6 May I wash my hands, please?

Ex 2 (student's own answers from table)

Ex 3 1 Rose may go to Arizona next year.   2 She may
ask for a month's holiday.   3 Her boss may not let her
go.   4 Rose/She may leave her job.   5 It may be
difficult to find another.   6 Rose/She may not want
another job in England.   7 She may stay in Arizona.
8 Nick and Rose/they may get married.   9 Jan may
never see Rose/her again.   **Ex 4** (student's own answers)

PAST PROGRESSIVE

Ex 1 1 He was studying art.   2 Kate was teaching
music.   3 They were sharing a flat.   4 He was
studying engineering.   5 He was working in a bank.
6 They were studying art.

Ex 2 1 Was Kate teaching music or art? She was teaching
music. She wasn't teaching art.   2 Were Nick and Rose
studying art or music? They were studying art. They
weren't studying music.   3 Was Tom working in a bank
or (in) a shop? He was working in a bank. He wasn't
working in a shop.   4 Were Kate and Rose sharing a flat
or a house? They were sharing a flat. They weren't
sharing a house.   5 Was Rose studying or teaching? She
was studying. She wasn't teaching.

Ex 3 A She took some photographs. She got into the
river. She tried to find her camera. She hurried home.
They talked. B She dropped her camera. She fell. A bee
stung her. She met a friend. She lost her keys. 1 While
she was taking some photographs, she dropped her
camera.   2 As she was getting into the river, she fell.
3 When she was looking for her camera, a bee stung her.
4 As she was hurrying home, she met a friend.
5 While they were talking, she lost her keys.

Ex 4 (student's own answers)

IF (Conditional 1)

Ex 1 1 The river.   2 The railway station.   3 The Star
Hotel.   4 The Sports Centre.   5 The market.   6 The
cinema.   7 The bus station.

Ex 2 1 If you turn right, you'll see it in front of you.
2 If you go straight ahead, you'll see it on your left.

3 If you turn left, you'll see it on your right.   4 If you turn left, you'll see it in front of you.   5 If you turn right, you'll see it on your left.

Ex 3   1 if you stay in your car.   2 if you touch the wires.   3 if you smoke.   4 if you open the gate.   5 if you swim.   6 if you fish.

Ex 4   1 I'll give...if you pass   2 you don't pass...you'll have to   3 I'll buy you...if you say   4 You'll miss...if you don't hurry!   5 If you're not/aren't...you won't be able   6 You'll fall if you're not/aren't

WOULD

Ex 1   1 Would you like to play...this afternoon?
2 Would you like to go to/eat in a...this evening?
3 Would you like to...tomorrow?   4 Would you like to...on Sunday? (*Then own answers*)

Ex 2   (*student's own answers*)

Ex 3   1 Would you open the window, please?
2 Would you lend me some money/(sum in local currency), please?   3 Would you post my letters, please?   4 Would you buy (me) four stamps, please?
5 Would you give me the newspaper, please?   6 Would you phone again later, please?

Ex 4   (*student's own answers following box and naming appropriate items*)

Ex 5, Ex 6   (*student's own answers according to patterns given*)

IF (Conditional 2)

Ex 1 and Ex 2   (*student's own answers*)

Ex 3   1 if I saw a burglar.   2 he had a gun.   3 he pointed the gun at me.   4 the burglar left without hurting me.   5 the police were too late.

Ex 4   1 If my cousin had a baby, I'd say 'Congratulations!'   2 If I stood on someone's foot by mistake, I'd say 'Oh, I'm very sorry.'   3 If someone gave me a present, I'd say 'Thank you very much.'   4 If I wanted to go past someone in the cinema, I'd say 'Excuse me, please.'   5 If I met someone for the first time, I'd say 'How do you do?'   6 If my friend was very unhappy about an exam, I'd say 'Don't worry about it.'

Ex 5   1 I'd buy a...if I were you.   2 I'd paint it...if I were you.   3 I'd go to...if I were you.   5 I'd see...if I were you.   6 I'd have...if I were you.

Ex 6   1 went, 'd/would go   2 'd/would visit, went
3 stayed, 'd/would spend   4 wouldn't be able, spent
5 was, wouldn't speak   6 would be, didn't try

EXCLAMATIONS

Ex 1   1 What an idea! It's in the middle of a desert.
2 What fun! We can swim every day.   3 What luck! You always win prizes.   4 What a lie! He probably spent it.   5 What a disappointment! Why aren't you going?   6 What a coincidence! That's *my* birthday, too.

Ex 2   (*student's own answers following example/box*)

SO/SUCH

Ex 1   1 so easy that everyone knows the answer.   2 so fierce that everyone is afraid of it.   3 so old that I'm going to throw it away.   4 so heavy that we can't lift it.
5 so expensive that I'm not going to buy it.   6 so cold that you need a scarf.

Ex 2   1 so many books   2 so much money   3 so

many children   4 so much rain   5 so many flowers

Ex 3   1 such warm water.   2 such a pretty village.
3 such friendly people.   4 such cheap restaurants.
5 such delicious food.   6 such a comfortable hotel.
7 such busy beaches.   8 such hot sand.

Ex 4   1 so   2 so   3 such   4 so   5 so   6 so
7 such   8 so   9 so   10 such   11 so   12 so
13 such   14 so

PAST PERFECT

Ex 1   1 A   2 A   2 B   3 B   4 B   5 A   6 B   7 A   8 B   9 A

Ex 2   1 The rain had already started when I reached home.   2 The phone had already started to ring when I opened the door.   3 It had stopped ringing when I reached it./I didn't reach it until it had stopped ringing.

Ex 3   1 When his father died, Peter had already found a job.   2 When we bought our new house, we sold the old one.   3 When Mary went to Paris, she had started French.   4 When the police arrived, the burglar escaped.

Ex 4   1 If only they had come sooner.   2 If only you had left home earlier.   3 If only you had walked more quickly.   4 If only you had got up earlier.   5 If only you had planned things better. (NOTE in items 2–5, answers with *I* are also acceptable)

Ex 5   (*student's own answers*)

MUST/CAN'T (LOGICAL)

Ex 1   1 must   2 can't   3 must   4 can't   5 must
6 must   7 can't   8 must   9 must   10 can't

Ex 2   1 They must mean, They can't mean   2 They can't mean, They must mean   3 They must mean, They can't mean   4 They must mean, They can't mean
5 They can't mean, They must mean

Ex 3   1 It can't be Chinese or American, because they aren't places   2 It can't be Canada or Greece, because they aren't cities.   3 It can't be Paris or Rome, because they don't have six letters.   4 It can't be Madrid or Athens, because they aren't in England.   5 It can't be London, so it must be Oxford!

INDIRECT STATEMENTS

Ex 1   1 She says she's coming on Sunday.   2 She says she's coming by train.   3 She says she'll get a taxi.
4 She says she's going to bring her cats/them.   5 She says she's been shopping.   6 She says she bought a new dress.   7 She says she hopes everyone's well, and she says she's looking forward to seeing us.
Ex 2   1 No, it isn't true that...   2 Yes, it's true that...
3 No, it isn't true that...   4 Yes, it's true that...
5 No, it isn't true that...   6 Yes, it's true that...

Ex 3   1 they were leaving   2 the next day   3 had phoned   4 the day before   5 she would send

Ex 4   1 they were taking the nine o'clock plane.
2 she'd have to get up early.   3 she didn't really like travelling by air.   4 it was the easiest way to travel.
5 they were going to spend a week in Paris.   6 she wanted to go up the Eiffel Tower.   7 they had been to Paris before.   8 they hadn't seen everything.
9 she'd/would send me a postcard.   10 she wouldn't write me a letter.   11 she was very excited.   12 they would be in Paris the next day.

Ex 5   1 I thought that he could swim.   2 I thought that he would help (me).   3 I thought that he could cook.   4 I thought that he could count.   5 I thought that he would drive.   6 I thought that he could speak French.   7 I thought that he would send you a postcard.

Ex 6   1 He said I ought to stay in bed.   2 He said I could get up for half an hour.   3 He said I could leave here on Thursday.   4 He said I ought to take some exercise.   5 He said I shouldn't walk too much.   6 He said I mustn't run at all.   7 He said I couldn't go back to work for a month.

USED TO

Ex 1   1 She used to be patient.   2 She used to be good-tempered.   3 She used to be fat.   4 She used to be pleasant.   5 She used to be friendly.   6 She used to be happy.

Ex 2   1 She never used to smoke.   2 She never used to drive very fast.   3 She never used to lose her temper. 4 She never used to shout.   5 She never used to arrive late.

Ex 3   1 He used to be fat.   2 He used to live in Britain. 3 She used to have long hair.   4 She used to find it difficult.   5 He used to have a cat.

WILL HAVE

Ex 1   1 By 8.45 tomorrow we'll have left home.   2 we'll have arrived at the airport.   3 we'll have taken off. 4 we'll have reached Paris.   5 we'll have left Paris. 6 we'll have arrived.

Ex 2   1 No, I don't think they'll have left home yet. 2 Yes, I expect they'll have left by now.   3 No, I don't think they'll have arrived at the airport yet.   4 Yes, I expect they'll have got on to the plane by now.   5 No, I don't think they'll have reached Paris yet.   6 Yes, I expect they'll have reached Paris by now.   7 Yes, I expect they'll have left Paris by now.

SHOULD HAVE

Ex 1   1 They should have got on to the plane at 9.45. 2 They should have taken off at 10.   3 They should have reached Paris at 11.   4 They should have left Paris at 12.30.   5 They should have arrived at 2.30. (NOTE times can also be expressed in words: eg *two thirty*)

Ex 2   1 I shouldn't have borrowed it. I should have asked first.   2 I shouldn't have eaten it. I should have washed it first.   3 I shouldn't have taken it. I should have asked for permission first.   4 I shouldn't have bought it. I should have tried it on first.   5 I shouldn't have gone (to the cinema). I should have told my mother/her first.

WOULD HAVE

Ex 1   (*student chooses affirmative or negative*)
1 would(n't) have stopped   2 would(n't) have screamed   3 would(n't) have given   4 would(n't) have told   5 would(n't) have been

Ex 2   (*student's own answers with* would(n't) have)

IF (Conditional 3)

Ex 1   1 he wouldn't have found such a good job. 2 she could have gone to America.   3 he might not have become the manager.   4 he would have stayed there.   5 she might have been an art teacher.   6 Rose couldn't have shared it with her.

Ex 2   1 John didn't work. He failed his exams.   2 The car had a puncture. We missed the train.   3 Jan bought

it. It was very cheap.   4 I didn't know. I didn't tidy it. 5 Rose went to the dentist. She had a hole in her tooth.

Ex 3   1 had been, wouldn't have sunk.   2 would have survived, had been   3 hadn't been able, would have drowned.   4 have escaped, had gone back   5 hadn't been, would have died.   **Ex 4**   (*student's own answers*)

PASSIVE

Ex 1   1 Bicycles are ridden by cyclists.   2 Trains are driven by engine drivers.   3 Buses are driven by bus drivers.   4 Planes are flown by pilots.   5 Taxis are driven by taxi drivers.   6 Lorries are driven by lorry drivers.

Ex 2   1 Columbus discovered America. America was discovered by Columbus.   2 *War and Peace* was written by Tolstoy. Tolstoy wrote *War and Peace*.   3 Alexander Graham Bell invented the telephone. It was invented by Alexander Graham Bell.   4 It was explored by Burton. Burton explored it.   5 The Pyramids were built by Egyptians. Egyptians built them.   6 It was discovered by Pierre and Marie Curie. Pierre and Marie Curie discovered it.

Ex 3   1 are chosen   2 are requested by   3 are ordered from a   4 are ordered   5 are read by   6 are covered 7 is given   8 be borrowed   9 are lost   10 are found   11 be borrowed   12 are sold   13 are given away   14 are thrown out

Ex 4   1 Fruit is grown in the south.   2 Oil is found in the north.   3 Bananas are grown in the south.   4 Gold is found in the west.   5 Diamonds are found in the east. 6 Pineapples are grown in the south.

Ex 5 and Ex 6   (*student's own answers following table*)

Ex 7   1 Gloria enjoys being photographed.   2 John hates/doesn't like being beaten at tennis.   3 Tom hates/doesn't like being called a fool.   4 Bill enjoys being interviewed on television.   5 Jan doesn't like being stopped by the police.   6 Kate doesn't like being phoned at midnight.

Ex 8   (*student's own answers following table*)

DEFINING RELATIVE CLAUSES

Ex 1   She's the person + 1 who invited me to Cambridge.   2 whose father is a professor.   3 who has a flat near the river.   4 whose flat is very modern. 5 whose brother works in Canada.   6 who came here once.   7 who works in the library.   8 whose car was stolen at Christmas.   9 who cycles to work now.

Ex 2   1 whose   2 who's   3 whose   4 who's 5 who's   6 whose   7 who's   8 whose

Ex 3   1 She's the girl I told you about.   2 She's the girl I was visiting last week.   3 She's the girl I stayed with. 4 She's the girl I've known for fifteen years.   5 She's the girl I used to share a flat with.   6 She's the girl I've invited here.   7 She's a girl I'm going to the theatre with tomorrow. (NOTE *that* is optional is every answer)

Ex 4   1 B   2 B   3 A   4 B   5 A   6 B

Ex 5   1 It's the film which is a true story about lions. 2 It's the film (which/that) I saw with Rose.   3 It's the film (which/that) I told you about.   4 It's the film (which/that) Angela saw on television.   5 It's the film (which/that) she liked.   6 It's the film (which/that) was made in East Africa.   7 It's the film (which/that) I enjoyed very much.

Ex 6 1 Paris is a city where there are many museums.
2 Rome is a city where the food is very good.
3 Athens is a city where there is a lot to see.
4 London is a city where there are hundreds of tourists.   5 New York is a city where there are a lot of skyscrapers.   6 Canada is a country where there are very cold winters.

Ex 7 (*student's own answers*)

Ex 8 1 where   2 that/which   3 (that/which)
4 who   5 whose   6 who   7 whose   8 whose   9 who

INDIRECT QUESTIONS

Ex 1 1 He wants to know what the man's name is.
2 He wants to know what his job is.   3 He wants to know where he works.   4 He wants to know where he lives.   5 He wants to know where he was yesterday.
6 He wants to know why he is in London.   7 He wants to know when he came.   8 He wants to know how he came.   9 He wants to know where his ticket is.

Ex 2 They asked if + 1 I was in Bristol yesterday.
2 I'd/had ever been in Bristol.   3 I knew anyone in Bristol.   4 I was in prison last month.   5 I'd/had ever been in prison.   6 I'd/had just escaped from prison.
7 I wanted to go back to prison.   8 I was telling the truth.   9 I could prove it.

Ex 3 He didn't know + 1 what to say.   2 how to answer.   3 how to prove it.   4 what to tell them.
5 whose name to give them.   6 how to convince them.

Ex 4 I wonder + 1 where Tom can be.   2 if the train's/is late.   3 if he has arrived yet.   4 why he hasn't phoned.   5 if he's/has gone to the bank.   6 why he's/is so late.   7 if he'll/will arrive soon.   8 when he'll/will come.

Ex 5 1 Siam   2 Russia/USSR   3 Helsinki   4 1492
5 St. Petersburg   6 England

INDIRECT COMMANDS AND REQUESTS

Ex 1 She told them + 1 to close the windows.   2 not to panic.   3 to walk slowly.   4 to go down the back stairs.   5 not to hurry.   6 to leave the room quietly.
7 to shut all the doors.   8 wait outside.   9 to go back to their classrooms.   10 not to run.   11 to walk.

Ex 2 1 When I was told to drive slowly, I drove fast.
2 When I was told to turn right, I turned left.   3 When I was told to drive forward, I reversed.   4 When I was told to turn after the bus stop, I turned before the bus stop.   5 When I was told to turn left, I turned right.

Ex 3 They asked me to + 1 tell them my name.
2 answer some questions.   3 wait for the nurse.
4 take my jacket off.   5 lie down.   6 lie still.   7 drink a cup of tea.   8 come/go back soon.

Ex 4 1 She told him to stop.   2 He asked them to turn it down.   3 He asked her to tell him the time.   4 She told him to ask someone else.   5 He told her to remember to write.   6 She asked him to help her.

PREPOSITIONS

Ex 1 1 for   2 without   3 at   4 of   5 for   6 with
7 in   8 at   9 to   10 for   11 like

Ex 2 1 at   2 in   3 from   4 of   5 for   6 out of
7 at   8 about   9 for   10 to   11 in   12 with

PHRASAL VERBS

Ex 1 1 Well, look it up, then. And when you've looked it up, write it down.   2 Have you tried it on? I'll put it on   3 why don't you take it down, Put it up   4 turn it down, like you to put it off.   5 put it down Well, pick it up,

Ex 2 1 broken down.   2 take off   3 going up, come down   4 put the fire out.   5 grown out of, give them away, throw them out.

NON-DEFINING RELATIVE CLAUSES

Ex 1 1 . . .Greece, which is a country with a long history.   2 . . .Athens, which is an interesting and historic city.   3 . . .islands, which are quiet, beautiful place.   4 . . .Andreas, who is a tourist guide.
5 . . .house, which is very pretty.   6 . . .family, who are all very friendly people.   7 . . .meal, which is always delicious.   8 . . .friends, who are very hospitable, too.

Ex 2 1 who   2 who   3 whom   4 who   5 who
6 whom   7 who   **Ex 3** (*student's own answers*)

QUESTION TAGS AND SHORT ANSWERS

Ex 1 1 doesn't she?   2 she does.   3 does she?
4 she doesn't.   5 can't she?   6 she can.   7 aren't they?'   8 they are.   9 haven't they?   10 have
11 did they?   12 they didn't.   13 didn't they?
14 they did.   15 isn't she?   16 she is.   17 isn't she?   18 she is.   19 did she?   20 she didn't.
21 doesn't she?   22 she does.   23 won't she?   24 she will.   25 will she?   26 she won't.   27 hasn't she?
28 she has.   29 doesn't she?   30 she does   31 isn't it?   32 it is.

Ex 2 1 Has she really!   2 Is she really!   3 Are they really!   4 Has he really!   5 Do they really!   6 Will she really!

TOO/EITHER

Ex 1 (*student's own answers*)

Ex 2 1 doesn't, either.   2 isn't either.   3 can't either.   4 doesn't, either.   5 isn't, either.

SO/NEITHER

Ex 1 1 So does Anna.   2 So do Anna and George.
3 So does Maria.   4 So do Maria and Ben.   5 So does Ben.

Ex 2 and Ex 3 (*student's own answers*)

INDIRECT STATEMENTS

1 Tell your parents what Aunt Nora says

DIRECT	INDIRECT
'I'm coming on Sunday.' 'I hope everyone's well.' 'I'll get a taxi.'	She says she's coming on SUNDAY. She says she hopes everyone's well. She says she'll get a taxi.

> I'm coming to see you on Sunday, and I'm coming by train. I'll get a taxi from the station. I'm going to bring my cats. I've been shopping and I bought a new dress. I hope everyone's well. Looking forward to seeing you.
> Love,
> Aunt Nora

1 When is Aunt Nora coming?

She says she's coming on Sunday.

2 And how?

_____

3 How will she come from the station?

_____

4 What about her cats?

_____

5 What's she been doing?

_____

6 What did she buy?

_____

7 What else does she say?

_____

_____

2 Are these things true?

> Yes, it's true that . . .
> No, it isn't true that . . .

1 The moon is made of cheese.

_____

2 The world is round.

_____

3 It's always sunny in England.

_____

4 Elephants eat grass and leaves.

_____

5 Whales eat people.

_____

6 People can live for a month without eating.

_____

Do they?

3 Read this and complete the table

DIRECT		INDIRECT
PETER	When are you going?	
JANE	*We're leaving tomorrow.*	Jane told Peter *they were leaving the next day.*
	I phoned you yesterday.	She said *she had phoned him the day before.*
PETER	Sorry, I wasn't at home.	
	Will you send me a postcard?	
JANE	Yes, of course *I will.*	She said *she would send* him a postcard.

DIRECT	We're leaving	tomorrow	phoned	yesterday	I will send
INDIRECT AFTER *said,* *told him*	1 *they were leaving*	2	3	4	5

4 Write sentences about Jane's trip to Paris

1 We're taking the nine o'clock plane.
   Jane told me *they were taking the nine o'clock plane.*

2 I'll have to get up early.
   She said _____

3 I don't really like travelling by air.
   She told me _____

4 But it's the easiest way to travel.
   But she decided _____

5 We're going to spend a week in Paris.
   She told me _____

6 I want to go up the Eiffel Tower.
   She said _____

7 We've been to Paris before.
   She told me _____

8 But we didn't see everything.
   But she said _____

9 I'll send you a postcard.
   She said _____

10 But I won't write you a letter.
    But she told me _____

11 I'm very excited!
    She said _____

12 We'll be in Paris tomorrow!
    The last thing she said was that _____

5 Write sentences to complete the conversation

DIRECT	INDIRECT	
He can't swim. He won't help.	I thought that he	could swim. would help.

1 KATE   You say you're going on holiday with Peter. Well, don't take him swimming. He can't swim.

   DON   *I thought that he could swim.* _____

2 KATE   And don't expect him to help you. He won't.

   DON   _____

3 KATE   No. You'll have to do all the cooking. He can't cook.

   DON   _____

4 KATE   And don't let him pay the bills. He can't count.

   DON   _____

5 KATE   And another thing: he won't drive, you know, not in France.

   DON   _____

6 KATE   And I hope you can speak French. Peter can't.

   DON   _____

7 KATE   Well, anyway, have a good holiday. And send me a postcard. Peter won't.

   DON   _____

   He is your brother, after all.

6 Tell your family what the doctor said

DIRECT	can	must	should	ought to
INDIRECT	could	must	should	ought to

1 You really ought to stay in bed,   *He said I ought to stay in bed.* _____

2 but you can get up for half an hour. _____

3 You can leave here on Thursday. _____

4 You ought to take some exercise. _____

5 But you shouldn't walk too much. _____

6 You mustn't run at all. _____

7 You can't go back to work for a month. _____

USED TO

1 Rose's boss has changed

She used to be . . .

1 She's impatient now.   *She used to be patient.*

2 She's bad-tempered.

3 She's thin.

4 She's unpleasant.

5 She's unfriendly.

6 She's unhappy, Rose thinks.

2 What else is different?

She never used to . . .

1 She smokes.   *She never used to smoke.*

2 She drives very fast.

3 She loses her temper.

4 She shouts.

5 She arrives late.

3 How have these people changed?

NOW   5 YEARS AGO

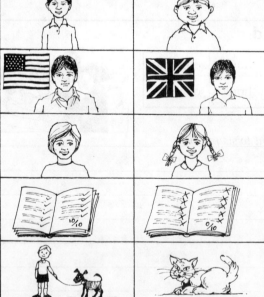

1 Bob's thin now.
  He used to be fat.

2 Nick lives in America now.

3 Jan has short hair.

4 Maria finds English easy.

5 Peter has a dog now.

34

WILL HAVE

1 Write sentences

| By this time tomorrow we'll have | left. |
| | arrived. |

It's Wednesday. Maria's grandparents are coming to visit her, and they're leaving tomorrow. Her grandmother has made a timetable.

She's thinking about tomorrow.

```
8.30  leave home          11.00  reach Paris
9.00  arrive at the airport  12.30  leave Paris
9.45  get on to the plane   14.30  arrive
10.00 take off
```

1   By 8.45 tomorrow   _we'll have left home._

2   By 9.10 we _____

3   By 10.15 _____

4   By 11.15 _____

5   By one o'clock _____

6   By three o'clock _____

2 Answer Maria's questions

| No, I don't think they'll have left home yet. |
| Yes, I expect they'll have left by now. |

Now, it's Thursday, and Maria is asking a lot of questions.

1   7.00   Have they left home yet?
        No, I don't think they'll have left home yet.

2   8.35   Now have they left?
        Yes, I expect they'll have left by now.

3   8.40   Have they arrived at the airport yet?

        _____

4   9.50   Have they got on to the plane yet?

        _____

5   10.00   Have they reached Paris yet?

        _____

6   11.10   Now have they reached Paris?

        _____

7   13.00   Have they left Paris yet?

        _____

SHOULD HAVE

1 What should have happened?

They The plane	should have	reached Paris at eleven. taken off at ten.

Remember Maria's grandparents' plan:

8.30 Leave home	11.00 reach Paris
9.00 arrive at the airport	12.30 Leave Paris
9.45 get on to the plane	14.30 arrive
10.00 take off	

1 At 10.30 they still hadn't got on to the plane.
They should have got on to the plane at 9.45.

2 At 12.15 they still hadn't taken off.

3 At 13.15 they reached Paris. (They missed the other plane, of course.)

4 They left Paris on a different plane at four o'clock.

5 They finally arrived at seven o'clock!

All the things that should have happened *didn't* happen!

2 What should you or shouldn't you have done?

I shouldn't have borrowed it. I should have asked first.

1 You borrowed a book without asking. Your friend was angry.
I shouldn't have borrowed it. I should have asked first.

2 You ate some fruit without washing it. You felt sick.

3 Without asking for permission, you took a photograph in a museum.

4 You bought a shirt without trying it on. It doesn't fit you.

5 After school you went to the cinema with some friends. Your mother was angry, because you didn't tell her.

WOULD HAVE

1 Would you have done the same thing?

| I would have stopped, too. |
| I wouldn't have stopped. |

Late one evening. Jan decided to go for a walk. A man came up to her on the street. She stopped.

1 _____

He took out a gun. She screamed.

2 _____

He said he wanted her money. She gave it to him.

3 _____

He said 'Don't tell the police.' But she told them.

4 _____

They arrested him the next day. Jan was glad.

5 _____

2 What would you have done?

1 Rose went shopping yesterday in Cambridge. A man came up to her in the street. He wanted her to help him to choose a hat for his wife! Rose didn't know whether to help or not.

I _____

2 Then Rose saw a child who wanted to cross the road. The child didn't see a motorbike that was coming. Rose didn't know whether to shout to the child or the motor-cyclist.

_____

3 After that Rose saw her boss in a shop. She was having a loud argument with the shop assistant. Rose didn't know whether to stop and say hello or not.

_____

4 Finally Rose finished her shopping and went home. When she reached her flat, she couldn't find her keys. Rose didn't know what to do: phone the police or break a window.

_____

IF (CONDITIONAL 3)

If + PAST PERFECT	*would/could/might* + *have* —*ed*
If Rose had gone to America,	she would have liked it.
If Nick had asked her sooner,	she could have gone.
If he had wanted her to stay,	she might have agreed.

1 Finish these sentences

> he wouldn't have found such a good job.
> she might have been an art teacher.
> she could have gone to America.
> Rose couldn't have shared it with her.
> he would have stayed there.
> he might not have become the manager.

1 Nick went to America, and found a very good job. If he had stayed in England,
he wouldn't have found such a good job.

2 He asked Rose to visit him, but she had already arranged to go to Italy. If she hadn't booked her holiday, ―――――――――――――――――――――――――――

3 Tom didn't want to go and work in a small bank in the north of England. But if he hadn't gone, ――――――――――――――――――――――――――――――――

4 Per got a job in Oslo. He didn't like it, so he left. If he had liked it,

――――――――――――――――――――――――――――――――――――――

5 If Rose hadn't become a photographer,

――――――――――――――――――――――――――――――――――――――

6 Jan's flat in Cambridge is quite big. If she had lived in a very small flat.

――――――――――――――――――――――――――――――――――――――

2 Which sentences are true?

1 If John had worked, he wouldn't have failed his exams.
John worked.
√ John didn't work.
√ He failed his exams.
He didn't fail his exams.

2 If the car hadn't had a puncture, we would have caught the train.
The car had a puncture.
It didn't have a puncture.
We caught the train.
We missed the train.

3 If that dress hadn't been so cheap, Jan wouldn't have bought it.

> Jan bought it.
> Jan didn't buy it.
> It was very cheap.
> It wasn't cheap.

4 If I'd known you were coming, I'd have tidied the living room.

> I knew you were coming.
> I didn't know.
> I tidied the living room.
> I didn't tidy it.

5 If Rose hadn't had a hole in her tooth, she wouldn't have gone to the dentist.

> Rose went to the dentist.
> She didn't go.
> She had a hole in her tooth.
> She didn't have a hole.

3 Complete the story with the verbs in brackets

1 If the captain ___*had been*___ more (be)

careful, the ship ___*wouldn't have sunk.*___ . (not sink)

2 More people _____ (survive)

if there _____ more lifeboats. (be)

3 If James _____ to swim, (not be able)

he _____ (drown)

4 And he might not _____ (escape)

if he _____ for his clothes. (go back)

5 If there _____ such a bad storm, (not be)

fewer people _____ . (die)

4 What would you have said or done?

. . . if someone had asked you to lend them some money yesterday?

_____

. . . if someone had invited you to London for a month?

_____

. . . if someone had offered you a job in a car factory?

_____

. . . if someone had asked you to be in a film?

_____

PASSIVE

1 These sentences have to be rewritten!

1 Bicycles are driven by taxi drivers.

Bicycles are ridden by cyclists.

2 Trains are flown by cyclists.

3 Buses are driven by engine drivers.

4 Planes are driven by bus drivers.

5 Taxis are ridden by lorry drivers.

6 Lorries are driven by pilots.

2 Write two answers (one active and one passive)

1 Who discovered America?

Columbus   *discovered America.*

America   *was discovered by Columbus.*

2 Who was *War and Peace* written by?

War and Peace _____

Tolstoy _____

3 Who invented the telephone?

Alexander Graham Bell _____

It _____

4 Who was Central Africa explored by?

It _____

Burton _____

5 Who built the Pyramids?

The Pyramids _____

Egyptians _____

6 Who was radium discovered by?

It _____

Pierre and Marie Curie _____

3 Read this conversation

Pat is going to write an article about libraries. He's talking to Jay, the librarian.

PAT   How do you choose new books for the library?

JAY   We usually choose them from catalogues. Or sometimes readers request books.

PAT   So then you order them from a bookshop, do you?

JAY   That's right. And we sometimes order two or more copies of a very popular book.

PAT   What do you do when the books arrive? Read them?

JAY   Well, we don't have time to read all of them, but we read a few, yes. Before we put the books on the shelves we have to do quite a lot of work. We have to cover them to keep them clean. We give each book a number and write an index card for it. Then the books go on to the shelves.

PAT   And people borrow them.

JAY   Some books are more popular than others, of course. We have to repair books after a while.

PAT   What do you do?

JAY   It depends. Sometimes we give a book a new cover.

PAT   Do you lose a lot of books?

JAY   Some, yes, but not many. When we check the shelves, which we do quite often, we usually find that some books have disappeared. We find a few of them later on.

PAT   What happens to books which are very old and dirty, books that can't be borrowed any more?

JAY   We sell them, or we give them away, or we throw them out.

PAT   You sell them? Well, please let me know when you're having a sale! New books are so expensive nowadays.

Now complete these sentences from Pat's article

New books ¹___are___ _____chosen_____ from catalogues, or sometimes they ²_____

_____ _____ readers. Then the books ³_____ _____ _____

_____ bookshop. Sometimes two or more copies ⁴_____ _____ if the book is

very popular. When the books arrive, a few of them ⁵_____ _____ _____ the

library staff. They ⁶_____ _____ to keep them clean, and each book ⁷_____

_____ a number. Then the books are put on to the shelves and can ⁸_____

_____. Every year a number of books ⁹_____ _____, but some ¹⁰_____

_____ later on. Books which are very old can't ¹¹_____ _____ any

more, and these books ¹²_____ _____, or else they ¹³_____ _____

_____, or they ¹⁴_____ _____ _____.

4 Write sentences about this island

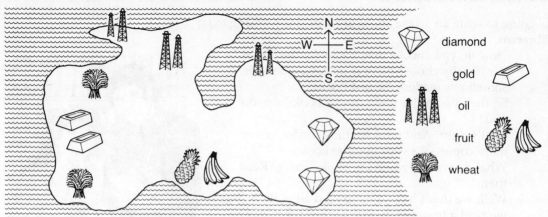

1 fruit/grow   *Fruit is grown in the south.*

2 oil/find   _____

3 bananas/grow   _____

4 gold/find   _____

5 diamonds/find   _____

6 pineapples/grow   _____

5 Give short answers about your country

1 Is gold found in your country? *Yes, it is./No, it isn't.* _____

2 Are oranges grown? _____

3 Is rice grown? _____

4 Are diamonds found? _____

5 Is oil found there? _____

6 Are coconuts grown? _____

6 What languages are used in your country?

A lot of Some A little	English Spanish . . .	is	spoken understood used	in education. in business. in hotels.

_____

_____

_____

_____

7 Find the person who . . .

. . .	enjoys doesn't like hates	being	photographed. beaten at tennis. telephoned at midnight. stopped by the police. called a fool. interviewed on television.

1 Gloria

enjoys being photographed.

2 John

_____

3 Tom

_____

4 Bill

_____

5 Jan

_____

6 Kate

_____

8 Do these things ever happen? Do you like them or not?

I like I don't like I don't mind	being told	I'm lazy.
I've never	been told	

Someone tells you you're lazy.

_____

Someone asks you to a breakfast party.

_____

Someone phones you at midnight.

_____

Someone asks you a silly question.

_____

Someone beats you at table tennis.

_____

Someone tells you you're stupid.

_____

Someone sends you flowers.

_____

DEFINING RELATIVE CLAUSES

1 Write about Maggie

She's the person	who	invited me to Cambridge. has a flat near the river.
	whose	father is a professor. car was stolen.

1 She invited me to Cambridge.

_____ *She's the person who invited me to Cambridge.* _____

2 Her father is a professor.

_____

3 She has a flat near the river.

_____

4 Her flat is very modern

_____

5 Her brother works in Canada.

_____

6 She came here once.

_____

7 She works in the library.

_____

8 Her car was stolen at Christmas.

_____

9 She cycles to work now.

_____

2 Whose or who's (who's = *who is* or *who has*)

1 Maggie's the girl ____*whose*____ father is a professor.

2 She's the person ____*who's*____ on the left in this photograph.

3 She's the girl _____ mother is French.

4 She's someone _____ always ready to help people.

5 She's a person _____ got hundreds of friends.

6 Maggie's someone _____ friends would do anything for her.

7 She's a person _____ always had a lot of close friends.

8 She's a girl _____ parents must be proud of her!

3 Who is Maggie?

She's the girl (that)	I told you about. I stayed with.

1 I told you about her.
She's the girl I told you about.

2 I was visiting her last week.

_____

3 I stayed with her.

_____

4 I've known Maggie for fifteen years.

_____

5 I used to share a flat with her.

_____

6 I've invited her here.

_____

7 I'm going to the theatre with her tomorrow.

_____

4 Read and choose the answer

Maggie's the girl . . .

1 . . . whose brother Jim lent £10.

A	Her brother lent Jim money.
✓ B	Jim lent him money.

2 . . . whose brother Rose drove to London.

A	Her brother drove Rose to London.
B	Rose drove him to London.

3 . . . whose brother asked us to a party.

A	Maggie's brother had a party.
B	We had a party.

4 . . . whose brother Angela saw at the cinema.

A	He saw Angela.
B	She saw him.

5 . . . whose brother taught Kate to play the guitar.

A	He taught her.
B	She taught him.

6 . . . whose brother Tom gave a job.

A	Maggie's brother gave Tom a job.
B	Tom gave him a job.

5 What do you know about *Claws*?

It's the film	which that	is about lions. was on TV last week.
	(which) (that)	I saw with Rose. I told you about.

1 It's a true story about lions.

   It's the film which is a true story about lions.

2 I saw it with Rose.

3 I told you about it.

4 Angela saw it on television.

5 She liked it.

6 It was made in East Africa.

7 I enjoyed it very much.

6 Write sentences

Rome	is a city where there	is	very good food.
Paris		are	many museums.

1 There are many museums in Paris.

   Paris is a city where there are many museums.

2 The food is very good in Rome.

3 In Athens there is a lot to see.

4 There are hundreds of tourists in London.

5 In New York there are a lot of skyscrapers.

6 In Canada there are very cold winters.

   country

7 Read about London

London has a long history.

Everyone has heard of London.

The streets of London are busy and exciting.

The shops are very good.

Many tourists visit London.

There are many exciting things to do.

Everyone can enjoy something in London.

LONDON IS:

a city which has a long history

a city everyone has heard of

a city whose streets are busy and exciting

a city whose shops are very good

a city many tourists visit

a city where there are many exciting things to do

a city where everyone can enjoy something

Now write some sentences about your town, city or country and finish the poster about it

_____

_____

_____

_____

_____

_____

8 Complete the conversation
(Sometimes you don't have to write anything!)

Angela is talking to Charlotte, a visitor from Sweden.

ANGELA   Have you been to St Paul's yet?

C'LOTTE   Do you mean the place ¹___where___ the royal wedding was?

ANGELA   That's right, the church ²_____ was designed by Christopher Wren.

C'LOTTE   Yes, I've been there. I've seen a lot of churches, but it's the one ³_____ I like best.

ANGELA   Who took you there? Or did you go alone?

C'LOTTE   No, I went with Louise. She's the girl ⁴_____ is at a language school. She's

the person ⁵_____ brother I met in Stockholm before I came here.

ANGELA   Was she the girl ⁶_____ got on to the wrong plane? Or the girl ⁷_____

passport was stolen? All your friends seem to have difficulties!

C'LOTTE   No, that wasn't Louise. She's a person ⁸_____ plans always work. She's the

girl I told you about ⁹_____ has just got a job in America.

INDIRECT QUESTIONS

1 | What does the policeman want to know?

DIRECT	INDIRECT	
What's your name? Where do you live?	The policeman wants to know	what the man's name is. where he lives.

1 What's your name?

    He wants to know what the man's name is.

2 What's your job?

    He wants to know what his job is.

3 Where do you work?

4 Where do you live?

5 Where were you yesterday?

6 Why are you in London?

7 When did you come?

8 How did you come?

9 Where's your ticket?

These are the man's answers: My name's Tom West. I'm a bank
manager. I work in Crossley, near Leeds, and I live there too. I was
there yesterday. I came to London to see my parents. I arrived this
afternoon, and I came by train – here's my ticket.
NO, I AM NOT A DANGEROUS CRIMINAL!
NO, I HAVEN'T JUST ESCAPED FROM PRISON!

2 What did the police ask? Write what Tom tells his parents

They asked if	I was in Bristol yesterday. I'd ever been in prison. I knew anyone in Bristol.

1 Were you in Bristol yesterday?
   They asked if I was in Bristol yesterday.

2 Have you ever been in Bristol?

3 Do you know anyone in Bristol?

4 Were you in prison last month?

5 Have you ever been in prison?

6 Have you just escaped from prison?

7 Do you want to go back to prison?

8 Are you telling the truth?

9 Can you prove it?

Tom told the police to talk to his boss in London. They did that, and shortly afterwards Tom was allowed to go.

3 Tom didn't know what to say

He didn't know	what to say. how to answer.

When Tom was in the police station, he was thinking these things:

1 What can I say?   *He didn't know what to say.*

2 How can I answer?

3 How shall I prove it?

4 What can I tell them?

5 Whose name shall I give them?

6 How can I convince them?

4 Write sentences with *I wonder*

While Tom was being questioned in the police station, his mother was wondering what had happened to him.

DIRECT	INDIRECT	
Where can Tom be	I wonder	where Tom can be.
Is the train late?		if the train's late.

1 Where can Tom be?
   I wonder where Tom can be.

2 Is the train late?

3 Has he arrived yet?

4 Why hasn't he phoned?

5 Has he gone to the bank?

6 Why is he so late?

7 Will he arrive soon?

8 Oh, when will he come?

5 Do you know . . . ?

1 Do you know what Thailand used to be called?   *Siam*

2 Do you know where Vladivostok is?

3 Do you know what the capital of Finland is?

4 Do you know when America was discovered?

5 Do you know what the old name for Leningrad was?

6 Do you know which is bigger, England or Scotland?

Write questions for your friend

Do you know where ———————————————

Do you know what ———————————————

Do you know when ———————————————

INDIRECT COMMANDS AND REQUESTS

1 What did their teacher tell them to do?

DIRECT	INDIRECT	
Close the windows! Don't run!	She told them	to close the windows. not to run.

Yesterday at school the fire alarm went.

1 Close the windows! *She told them to close the windows.*

2 Don't panic! *She told them not to panic.*

3 Walk slowly! _____

4 Go down the back stairs! _____

5 Don't hurry! _____

6 Leave the room quietly! _____

7 Shut all the doors! _____

8 Wait outside! _____

9 Go back to your classrooms! _____

10 Don't run! _____

11 Walk! _____

(Yes, it was only a practice. It wasn't a real fire. But if we didn't have practices, we wouldn't know what to do if there was a fire.)

2 When I was told to do something, I always did the opposite

OPPOSITES:	slowly fast	turn right turn left	to drive forward to reverse	after . . . before . . .

Don sat his driving test last week. But he didn't pass. He said he did everything wrong.

1 Drive slowly. *When I was told to drive slowly, I drove fast.*

2 Turn right. _____

3 Drive forward. _____

4 Turn after the bus stop. _____

5 Turn left. _____

51

3 What did they ask you to do?

They asked me to	tell them my name. answer some questions.

1 Now, if you'll just tell us your name, please?
They asked me to tell them my name.

2 And maybe you can answer some questions?
_____

3 Now will you wait for the nurse, please?
_____

4 Would you like to take your jacket off?
_____

5 Will you lie down, please?
_____

6 Good. Would you lie still, please?
_____

7 Now, can you drink a cup of tea?
_____

8 You will come back soon, won't you?
_____

(Do you know what was happening? Someone was giving blood.)

4 Did they TELL them to do it, or did they ASK them?

1 'Stop!'
She told him to stop.

2 'Will you turn it down, please?'
_____

3 'Can you tell me the time?'
_____

4 'I don't know. Go and try again'.
_____

5 'Remember to write.'
_____

6 'Would you help me, please?'
_____

PREPOSITIONS

1 Complete the conversation

DON Hurry up! I'm not going to wait ¹_*for*_ you any longer.

VAL Oh, please wait! Don't go ²_____ me. I'm looking for my umbrella. It's going to rain. Look ³_____ the sky.

DON Well, you aren't afraid ⁴_____ getting wet, are you?

VAL No, but I don't want to get my new jacket wet. I paid a lot of money ⁵_____ it last week. Ah, here's my umbrella.

DON A pink umbrella? With a yellow jacket? They don't go ⁶_____ each other, you know.

VAL Look, I want to keep dry. I'm not interested ⁷_____ looking beautiful.

DON Leave it ⁸_____ home. Who needs a pink umbrella?

VAL Listen ⁹_____ me! Either I take my umbrella or I don't go ¹⁰_____ a walk. It doesn't matter what I look ¹¹_____

2 Use these letters to find the missing words

A̶ A A B FFFFF H III M NN OO
OOOOOO RRR T̶ TTTTT UU W

These people are ¹_*at*_ London Airport. They've just arrived ²_____ England. They've come ³_____ Omaruru. (Where's that? I've never heard ⁴_____ Omaruru.) They're waiting ⁵_____ their luggage now.

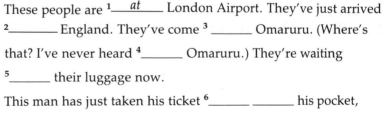

This man has just taken his ticket ⁶_____ _____ his pocket, and he's looking ⁷_____ it. He looks worried ⁸_____ something: his luggage?

He's going to meet his sister soon. They haven't seen each other ⁹_____ three years, and he's looking forward ¹⁰_____ seeing her again.

His sister is a doctor who works ¹¹_____ a big London hospital. She shares a flat ¹²_____ another doctor.

PHRASAL VERBS

1 Complete these sentences with verbs and pronouns

+ NOUN	+ PRONOUN
He put his hat on. He put on his hat.	He put it on.

1 Here's a word I don't know. Well, _____*look it up,*_____, then. And when you've

   _*looked it up,*_____, _*write it down.*_____.   (look up, write down)

2 Shall I buy this dress?

   Have _____?

   Not yet. I'll _____ and you can tell me what you think.   (try on, put on)

3 I don't like that picture on the wall.

   Well, why don't you _____, then? Here's another picture.

   _____ and see if you like it better.   (take down, put up)

4 Dad, can I turn up the music? It needs to be very loud.

   Loud? It's loud enough already. Please _____.

   In fact, I'd really like you to _____.   (turn down, put off)

5 Where's the newspaper?

   I _____ on the floor.

   Well, _____, please, and give it to me.   (put down, pick up)

2 Use these phrasal verbs to complete the sentences

break down	come down	give away	go up
grow out of	put out	take off	throw out

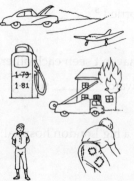

1 This car has _____*broken down.*_____.

2 That plane is ready to _____ now.

3 The price of petrol is _____ again.

   Well, prices don't often _____, do they?

4 I hope the firemen manage to _____ the fire _____.

5 Johnny has _____ these trousers.

   Perhaps he can _____ them _____.

   No, they're too old. He'll _____ them _____.

54

NON-DEFINING RELATIVE CLAUSES

1 Write sentences with *who* or *which*

. . .	Andreas, his friends,	who . . .

. . .	Athens, his house,	which . . .

1 Many tourists visit Greece.   (a country with a long history)

Many tourists visit Greece, which is a country with a long history.

2 Most tourists go to Athens.   (an interesting and historic city)

_____

3 Many visit the islands.   (quiet, beautiful places)

_____

4 If you go to Delos, you'll probably meet Andreas.   (a tourist guide)

_____

5 He'll ask you back to his house.   (very pretty)

_____

6 He'll introduce you to his family.   (all very friendly people)

_____

7 He'll give you a meal.   (always delicious)

_____

8 And you'll meet his friends.   (very hospitable, too)

_____

2 Complete these sentences with *who* or *whom*

Maria is a teacher. I liked Maria.	I met Maria, who is a teacher. I met Maria, whom I liked.

1 I'll give you a letter for Andreas, ____*who*____ helped me last year.

2 And I have a present for Maria, _____ is his wife.

3 Andreas introduced me to Maria, _____ I liked very much.

4 Their son Theo, _____ is eight, doesn't speak much English.

5 They also have a baby, Panos, _____ is always laughing.

6 But let me tell you more about Andreas, _____ I really admire.

7 Andreas, _____ left school when he was twelve, managed to teach himself English!

3 Read about Per's country

I come from Norway, which is in the north of
Europe. Norway, which has a small
population, is a fairly small country. The
capital is Oslo, which is in the south. Other
cities are Bergen (in the west) and Trondheim,
which is also in the west. We speak
Norwegian. English, which everyone learns at
school, is understood everywhere.

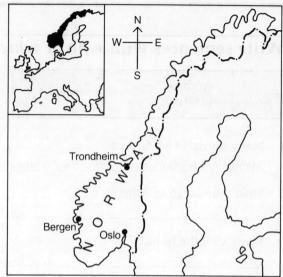

Make notes about your country

name? _____

north/south/east/west/centre of which continent? _____

population: (fairly) large/small? _____

size of country: (fairly) large/small? _____

capital? _____ where? _____

other cities: i) _____ where? _____ ii) _____ where? _____

language? _____

Who learns English: everyone? most/some people? _____

Is English understood: everywhere? in most/some/a few places?

Now write a similar paragraph about your country and draw a map

I come from _____

_____

_____

_____

_____

_____

_____

_____

QUESTION TAGS AND SHORT ANSWERS

1 Complete the questions and answers

SENTENCE	QUESTION TAG
affirmative	negative
negative	affirmative

Rose speaks Italian, [1] _doesn't she?_ _____ ?   Yes, [2] _she does._ _____ .

But she doesn't speak German, [3] _____ ?   No, I'm sure [4] _____ .

Kate can speak German, [5] _____ ?   Yes, [6] _____ .

In fact most of her friends are German,

[7] _____ ?   Yes, [8] _____

Some of them have visited England,

[9] _____ ?   Two of them [10] _____ , yes.

They didn't stay in a hotel, [11] _____ ?   No, [12] _____

They stayed with Kate's parents, [13] _____ ?   That's right, [14] _____ .

Kate's friend is called Ursula, [15] _____ ?   Yes, [16] _____ .

Ursula's going to Scotland this year, [17] _____ ?   Yes, [18] _____ .

She didn't go there last year, [19] _____ ?   No, [20] _____ .

She wants to go to Edinburgh, [21] _____ ?   Yes, [22] _____ .

She'll like it, [23] _____ ?   Yes, I expect [24] _____ .

But Kate won't be at home, [25] _____ ?   No, [26] _____ .

She's found a job in Bremen, [27] _____ ?   Yes, [28] _____ .

She hopes to make a lot of money, [29] _____ ?   I suppose [30] _____ , yes.

Living in Hamburg is expensive, [31] _____ ?   Yes, Kate says [32] _____ .

2 Show how surprised you are

STATEMENT	EXCLAMATION
affirmative	affirmative

1 Rose has given up her job.   _Has she really!_ _____

2 She's going to Arizona next week.   _____

3 She and Nick are going to get married.   _____

4 Nick has bought a house.   _____

5 And they think Rose can find a good job.   _____

6 She'll probably earn a lot of money.   _____

TOO/EITHER

1 Read about these people

George is a schoolboy. He lives in a city and goes to a large school. He's been learning English for three years. He likes playing football.

Maria is a schoolgirl. She lives in a town and goes to a small school. She enjoys swimming and learning English. She'd like to visit England. She's been abroad before.

Anna has a job. She works in a city. She speaks French and Spanish. She'd like to work in England or America.

Ben has left school. He's a student. He comes from a village. He works hard and he hopes to get a good job.

Which things are the same for you and for them?

Write about them and add a sentence about yourself:

I	am, do, have, would,	too.

George learns English.

I do, too.

2 Add sentences with *either*

. . .	isn't, doesn't, can't,	either.

1 George doesn't have a job.   Maria *doesn't, either*.

2 Ben isn't at school.   Anna

3 Anna can't play football.   Maria

4 Ben doesn't live in a village now. George

5 Maria isn't a university student.   George

58

SO/NEITHER

1 Write sentences

So	does	...
	do	...and...

1 George lives in a city. (Anna) *So does Anna.*

2 Maria likes swimming. (Anna and George) _____

3 Ben works hard. (Maria) _____

4 Anna wants to go to England. (Maria and Ben) _____

5 George likes football. (Ben) _____

2 Add sentences about people you know who are the same

Neither	does/do has/have would am/is/are can	....

1 George doesn't like getting up early. _____

2 Ben has never visited another country. _____

3 Anna wouldn't like to work in a village. _____

4 Maria isn't very good at history. _____

5 She can't remember things well. _____

3 Copy the sentences you agree with and add a sentence about yourself

So Neither	do	I.

Ben likes television.	Anna doesn't like television very much.
Anna speaks Spanish.	Ben doesn't speak Spanish.
Maria works hard.	George doesn't work very hard.

_____

_____

_____